A Mennonite
Statement and Study
on Violence

Study Guide by Lois Barrett

Faith & Life Press
Newton, Kansas
Winnipeg, Manitoba

Herald
Press

Herald Press
Scottdale, Pennsylvania
Waterloo, Ontario

About the cover:

The cover photo is a detail of the sculpture "Guns Into Plowshares," right, by Esther K. and Michael D. Augsburger of Harrisonburg, Virginia. The mother and son team built the steel structure using 3,000 hand-guns that had been confiscated by city police in Washington, D.C., to be melted down for other uses. The sculpture, says Michael Augsburger, "is a symbol of the hope that this city will share with the world a quest for peace." Dedicated in September 1997, the work stands in the city's Judiciary Square.

Cover photo by Esther K. Augsburger. Photo at right by Robert Maust Photography, Harrisonburg, Virginia.

Printed in the United States of America

International Standard Book Number 0-87303-339-6

Design by Ilene Franz
Printing by Mennonite Press, Inc., Newton, KS

Unless otherwise noted, Scripture text is from the New Revised Standard Version, copyright © 1990, Division of Christian Education of the National Council of the Churches of Christ in the United States of America.

Contents

Background on this booklet

How can the church respond to society's increasing concerns about violence? This question was part of the agenda at a 1994 meeting of the Council of Moderators and Secretaries, an association drawn from Anabaptist denominations. From there, the General Boards of the Mennonite Church and General Conference Mennonite Church appointed a committee of four to draft a statement. This statement was tested with area conference peace committees and the General Boards, and approved in principle by the delegate bodies of both denominations in summer, 1997. It was given final approval by the General Boards in joint session in November 1997.

What is the purpose of such a statement? One intent is to answer questions of those within and outside the church on what Mennonites believe about violence and nonviolence. But even more, the statement takes on meaning as congregations and church agencies make it their own and act on it.

With this in mind, Faith & Life Press commissioned an accompanying study-action guide (page 39) to be written by one of the statement's authors, Lois Barrett. The statement and study together give congregations, groups and individuals some handles for confronting the various forms of violence in our society, and even in our homes and churches.

This study-action guide is intended to be a tool for congregations and other groups to consider issues of violence and peacemaking and to discern how we can follow Christ's call to be peacemakers in a violent world.

Members of the Joint Committee on Violence:
    Florence Duley, Edmonton, Alberta
    Doug Pritchard, Toronto, Ontario
    Roger Steffy, Mechanicsburg, Pennsylvania
    Lois Barrett, Wichita, Kansas

And No One Shall Make Them Afraid

A Mennonite Statement on Violence

I. Introduction

Jesus came that we might have life and have it abundantly (John 10:10). However, violence, the threat of violence, and the fear of violence permeate life in North America, often robbing us of this abundant life. Violence is also pervasive in our world. Perpetrated by individuals, groups, social systems, and governments, it leaves countless victims around the globe.

As Mennonites in Canada, the United States, and Puerto Rico, we have been affected by this violence. While we affirm a commitment to peace and nonviolence, we have frequently tolerated and even benefited from some forms of violence. We have wrongly accepted, at least in part, what theologian Walter Wink has called the "myth of redemptive violence," the belief that good ends can come from violent means, and that some violence is necessary to solve problems, to ensure security, and to make peace.

The scope of this statement, while broad in some respects, is limited in several ways. The terms *violent* and *violence* refer only to violence perpetrated by human beings, human institutions, and human social structures, which harms human beings. The statement makes no attempt to address acts of God or human violence that harms animals or other parts of God's creation. While these are important issues, they are beyond the scope of this statement.

For the purpose of this statement, violence is defined as **the human exercise of physical, emotional, social, or technological power which results in injury or harm to oneself or others**. The perpetrators of violence often exploit an imbalance of power to dominate, control, or use others. The various kinds of violence form a continuum. At one end are acts of physical violence, rape, incest, and sexual abuse, which result in serious psychological damage, severe bodily injury, and/or death. At the other end are acts of intimidation, threats, and emotional and verbal abuse, which result in fear and the destruction of personhood.

Any form of human violence, wherever it might appear on the continuum, is an expression of evil. Violence was present in the first human family. Since then, the spirits of revenge, greed, and domination, along with unresolved anger, have multiplied violence many times. Violence alienates us from God and from each other, and the fear of violence is a prison in which our very souls shrivel.

All violence is fundamentally incompatible with the reign of Jesus Christ in God's kingdom of love. Therefore, as followers of Jesus Christ, the Prince of Peace, we must directly confront the reality of violence in and around us. Jesus calls us not to resist evil with violence and to forgive rather than to seek revenge. We want to find ways to reject all forms of violence in our relationships and endeavors, and to increase our efforts to live out the nonviolent way of Jesus.

This statement seeks to name the violence in ourselves, our church, and our society. It identifies ways in which the church is responding to this violence and suggests additional ways for us to respond as peacemakers and children of God.

II. Biblical and Theological Foundations

One of the most basic issues of the Bible is how one deals with evil, and with violence in particular. In spite of some Old Testament Scriptures where certain kinds of violence were used, the basic direction of both the Old and New Testaments is toward peacemaking, which includes nonretaliation, reconciliation, and mutuality.

God's intention for a peaceful world has been present since creation. Genesis 1 describes the creation of humankind, male and female, in God's own image. Both the woman and the man were blessed and given the command to fill the earth and subdue it. Both were given dominion over the rest of creation, but neither was given dominion over the other. This peaceful creation was marred by sin. The rule of man over woman is one of the consequences of sin (Gen. 3:16). This pattern of domination continues with Cain's murder of his brother Abel and with Lamech's song of revenge (Gen. 4). Then "the earth was filled with violence." This is one of the reasons given for the great flood in the time of Noah (Gen. 6:11).

One of the purposes of the Law (Torah) was to restrain violence and to provide penalties for violent behavior (including murder, rape, assault, and theft) within Israelite society. In the Prophets and Writings, violence is associated with many kinds of sin, including human bloodshed (Hab. 2:8), kidnapping (Hab. 1:9), injustice and unrighteousness (Isa. 59:6), planning evil things and stirring up wars (Ps. 140:1-2), wars of ruler against ruler (Jer. 51:46), eviction of people from their land (Ezek. 45:9), and robbery (Amos 3:10). For Isaiah, violence is the opposite of peace, justice, salvation, and the praise of God (Isa.59:6-8; 60:17-18). According to the Old Testament, the source of violence is not only the human heart, but the "gods," the spiritual powers that act contrary to the ways of the true God (Ps. 58:1-2).

War, as an act of mass violence of one nation against another, although sometimes sanctioned in the Old Testament, is restricted by God to old-fashioned weaponry (Isa. 31:1), to small armies (Judg. 7), and to dependence on God for victory (Judg. 7:2; Ps. 20:6-7). The Books of the Law, as well as the later Prophets, hold up as the ideal battle the crossing of the sea in the Exodus, when God fought for Israel, and Israel had no weapons (Exod. 14:13-14).

The Psalms, as well as other passages, expect that God will save people not only from the sins they commit, but also from violence committed against them (2 Sam. 22:3; Ps. 18:48; 140:1). One of the ways that God will take care of the violent and the wicked is to let their own violence turn back upon themselves (Ps. 7:16; 37:12-15; Prov. 21:7). God also brings salvation through surprising acts of deliverance: making a way through the Red Sea, or routing the enemy with floods and swarms of hornets (Exod. 14—15; Judg. 5:21; Josh. 24:12).

The Prophets look forward to the day when violence will be no more, when even the wolf, lion, and lamb will be at peace with one another (Isa.65:25). In the age to come, people will trust in God alone and "no one shall make them afraid" (Zeph. 3:12-13).

In the New Testament, Jesus suffers violence, but does not commit violence. Although Jesus at times chose to avoid suffering (Luke 4:28-30), he accepted suffering when his hour had come. Jesus told his followers not to use violence to prevent him from being arrested (Matt. 26:52; John 18:36), thus rejecting the use of violence for self-defense. He suffered crucifixion, but God overcame the violence by raising Jesus from the dead.

Jesus taught his disciples not only to avoid committing violence, but actively to love their enemies (Matt. 5:43ff.); not only to avoid murder or insult, but to be reconciled with the brother or sister (Matt. 5:21ff.); not only to avoid adultery or rape, but to refrain from looking on each other with lust (Matt. 5:27ff.). Instead, Jesus' followers are to respond to enemies with surprising acts of mercy and nonviolence—going the second mile, for example (Matt. 5:38-42).

As Jesus had forewarned them, the early disciples experienced persecution, imprisonment, banishment, beating, and execution. The apostle Paul was an intended victim of mob violence (Acts 21:35-36). Far from complaining about his imprisonment, Paul rejoiced no matter what his situation and considered that he and others like him were completing the sufferings of Christ, participating in Christ (Col. 1:24). Paul assumed that believers would no longer participate in such sin as murder and strife (Rom. 1:29-31). The general prohibitions against violence also appear in the qualifications for a bishop (1 Tim. 3:3; Tit. 1:7). The writings of the early church reinforce Jesus' teaching against retaliation and violence: "Do not repay evil for evil or abuse for abuse; but, on the contrary, repay with a blessing" (1 Pet. 3:9); "Beloved, never avenge yourselves, but leave room for the wrath of God. . . . Do not be overcome by evil, but overcome evil with good" (Rom. 12:19, 21). In the early centuries of the church, these teachings applied not only to personal morality; they informed those Christians who refused to participate in the army and its organized violence.

The examples of Jesus and the early church can give us guidance in not intending violence against others. Likewise, they show us how to deal with others' violence against us. We believe the following about violence and suffering:

1. God's wrath sometimes allows sin to boomerang against the sinner, but God's central attribute is love. God may turn suffering to our good or use it to teach us, but God does not desire that anyone suffer. In Jesus' healing ministry, he worked actively to relieve suffering. The powers of violence are active in the world and, in this age, sometimes thwart God's will. Only in the age to come, when Christ's victory over the powers (by means of the "sword of his mouth," that is, the Word) is apparent to all, will violence be completely overcome.

2. No violence committed against us, or those we love, justifies our committing violence in return. When we are sinned against, we become more vulnerable to the temptation to sin in return. But violence does not overcome violence; it only turns us also into violent people. There is no way to peace and nonviolence, except through peaceful, nonviolent means.

3. No suffering, not even death, can separate us from the love of God in Christ Jesus (Rom. 8:38-39; 2 Cor. 4:8-10). God, whose

own Son suffered and was killed, is with all those who suffer and call on God for help and comfort. No violent act committed against us can remove us from relationship with God. God's invitation "Do not be afraid" echoes through the Old and New Testaments. God helps us overcome our fears when we put ourselves completely into the hands of a loving God.

4. The process of forgiveness is the way to get through suffering. Forgiveness, in contrast to reconciliation, does not require the perpetrator's repentance. Instead, forgiveness is a process we go through in the power of the Holy Spirit to release and to begin loving the offender or enemy rather than harboring anger. Forgiveness is a choice not to become what we hate.

5. When we choose the way of loving enemies, rather than violence, we are becoming transformed into the image of Christ, who is the image of God. Romans 5:10 affirms that the character of God is one of love for us; even when we were God's enemies, Christ died for us. And Matthew 5:38-48 explains that it is precisely when we are loving enemies that we are acting as God acts. Our love may also open the way for God to transform enemies and situations of violence.

Thus, Christians are not to commit acts of violence nor to respond violently to enemies. Beyond this, Christians are called to be channels of God's peace and to help reconcile others who are committing violence against each other. Christ calls us not only to be gentle or nonviolent, but to be peacemakers, active workers for peace, inviting others to turn to Christ's way of love (Matt. 5:5, 9).

We affirm, with the *Confession of Faith in a Mennonite Perspective*, that "violence is not the will of God. We witness against all forms of violence, including war among nations, hostility among races and classes, abuse of children and women, violence between men and women, abortion, and capital punishment."[1]

III. Violence and Our Life Experiences

Violence is pervasive in many areas of life. In the following sections, violence and the church's response to it will be explored in five ever-widening circles of life experience, from individual to global. Each section includes calls for specific action. Even though no one

---

1. Article 22, "Peace, Justice, and Nonresistance," p. 82 (Scottdale, Pa.: Herald Press, 1995).

person or congregation will be able to do all these things at one time, we must remember that silence and inaction can perpetuate violence. We call the church to consider prayerfully how it will respond.

A. Violence Against Oneself. Jesus invites each person to enjoy wholeness. Resources to foster wholeness are available through the Holy Spirit, the Scriptures, and the church. However, instead of accepting this gift from God, we often commit violence against ourselves.

Suicide and attempted suicide are the ultimate violence against the self, but suicide leaves many other victims—family, friends, even whole congregations. Understandings gained from our mental health ministries are leading us into greater openness and helpfulness in these tragedies. As we practice compassionate care and listening, we can displace secrecy, fear, and condemnation, and we can provide safe places to grieve, talk, and struggle with difficult questions.

Another form of violence against self is violence for "kicks"—reckless risk-taking to prove oneself, demand respect, or achieve a high. Such recklessness can be manifested in many ways.

An additional, more subtle form of violence against self, abortion, not only ends the life of the unborn but violates the woman who has chosen it, or who has had this decision forced upon her. She will very likely feel she has lost a part of herself and will need to grieve the irreversible decision she has made. This can be a life-wrenching experience for the woman, sometimes for the father of the unborn, and others close to them.

There are numerous other forms of violence against the self, including substance abuse, eating disorders, and self-mutilation. Not all of these forms can be addressed here.

Self-destructive patterns often develop without any awareness of the harmful consequences to self and others. Such behaviors may result from individualism and selfish choices, from fear or unresolved anger, or from other interacting factors such as mental illness, trauma, major losses, or inadequate economic, emotional, or spiritual support. Often the self-destructive person has been the victim of another's violence. Part of the enslaving nature of evil is the cyclical pattern of violence in which victims become violators—becoming what they hate, and sometimes hating themselves, too.

In response to violence against oneself, we call the church to:
— counsel, nurture, and lead people away from behaving violently against themselves.

— *build each other up with affirmation, encouragement, and prayer.*

— *help people learn to process anger and rage in healthy ways.*

— *become better informed about depression, its early symptoms, and evaluation of suicide risk factors.*

— *encourage people to choose constructive, life-enhancing behavior rather than self-destructive behavior and harmful addictions.*

— *respond with compassion to all those hurt by abortion, seeking to help them in their journey of healing.*

— *be instruments of God's grace for forgiveness and healing, acknowledging that violence against the self, while contrary to the will of God, is also within the range of God's redemptive work.*

— *uphold the value of, and cherish, every human life.*

B. Violence in Close Relationships. As humans, we need close relationships. In our families and friendships, we love and care for one another, nurture children, and experience God's love. Yet, in these close relationships, many people experience intense personal violence.

Violence in close relationships takes many forms. It can be physical, sexual, verbal, or psychological. Most commonly it is perpetrated by men against women and children. However, some women also use violence against their partners and/or their children, some juveniles abuse their parents, and some adults abuse elderly parents.

Research reveals that spousal abuse occurs in more than one quarter of marriages in the United States and Canada, and that almost all of the victims are women.[2] Research also reveals that the incidence of family violence may be as high in Mennonite homes as in the general population.[3] We confess that, while we affirm a commitment to peace and nonviolence, many of us have allowed violence in our homes and in our churches.

Child abuse continues to be widespread. Through abortion, many children become victims before birth. In Canada and the

2. "What Every Congregation Needs To Know About Domestic Violence" (Seattle: Center for the Prevention of Sexual and Domestic Violence, 1994).

3. Isaac Block, *Assault on God's Image: Domestic Abuse.* Winnipeg: Windflower Communications, 1992.

United States, abortion results in over one million deaths each year.[4] Violence against children takes many forms, including physical abuse, incest and other types of sexual abuse, psychological and emotional abuse, threats and verbal abuse, and neglect and abandonment. Numerous studies show that rates of child abuse are alarmingly high. Those who work with survivors of childhood abuse testify that the same seems to be true in the church.

We acknowledge that sometimes it is necessary and appropriate physically to restrain children in order to protect them or others and/or to discipline them. Such restraint should always use the least amount of physical force possible and should be done to ensure safety, never to instill fear or to harm the child.

Physical and sexual violence in dating relationships among teens and young adults is also widespread. Statistics show that rape and attempted rape are major problems in this age group. Most of this sexual violence, as well as physical violence, is perpetrated on dates or by persons known to the victim.

Sexual misconduct by pastors, church leaders, and counselors also violates close, trusting relationships. This form of violence is present in the Mennonite church and may be more prevalent than we want to admit.

At the heart of nearly all violence in close relationships is the desire to control or use another person. This violence exploits some perceived or actual imbalance of power in the relationship, whereby the person with more power seeks to dominate the person with less power. The attempt to control may begin with verbal and emotional abuse such as put-downs and name calling. If these tactics do not work, some people resort to physical or sexual violence. As painful as this relationship may be, many are reluctant to leave an abusive relationship because they fear economic consequences and other factors.

According to the video *Broken Vows*,[5] churches have been slow to respond helpfully to violence in close relationships. Some victims of abuse have not been listened to or believed by their congregations. Sometimes victims have not received the support needed

---

4. According to the U.S. Centers for Disease Control and Prevention, and Health Canada.

5. *Broken Vows: Religious Perspectives on Domestic Violence* (Seattle, Wash.: Center for the Prevention of Sexual and Domestic Violence, 1994).

to leave an abusive situation and to seek healing. Sometimes victims have been blamed by well-meaning church leaders and told to go back to the abuser and be more submissive. Some congregations are beginning to respond more helpfully to victims. Yet, we have a long way to go in responding to both victim and abuser.

We affirm the congregations and church agencies that have begun to respond. The Women's Concerns Office of Mennonite Central Committee has provided educational materials, workshops, and a support network for survivors of abuse. Some area conferences have held workshops or appointed special committees to respond to abuse. Two consultations for Mennonite leaders called "Men Working To End Violence Against Women" helped participants begin to better understand the dynamics of power and control in close relationships, and called men to a new level of accountability and nonviolence.

Victims and perpetrators of violence in close relationships are not just someone else, somewhere else. When any congregation meets for worship, undoubtedly victims, survivors, and perpetrators of abuse are present. We need to start with honest self-reflection and a careful review of our own relationships, so that healing and change can begin with us and flow through us to a hurting world.

In response to violence in close relationships, we call the church to:

— *move beyond denial and disbelief, break the silence that surrounds domestic and professional abuse, and proclaim that the gospel of peace and nonviolence applies to close relationships.*

— *make the church a safe place for victims and survivors of abuse so that they may speak up and receive care and healing.*

— *promote and support compassionate and realistic alternatives to abortion.*

— *learn the special dynamics of power and control that are at work in violence within close relationships.*

— *recognize that the safety of the victim—whether adult or child—is the first priority, and that providing safety often requires a period of separation.*

— *recognize that individual counseling rather than counseling the couple together is essential for the safety, transformation, and healing of the domestic abuse victim.*

— *work redemptively in calling perpetrators to be accountable for their actions, to stop their violent behavior, and to submit to God in their own transformation and healing within the church.*
— *reexamine our understandings of church and home leadership in light of Jesus' teaching and example, and reject any patterns based on injustice.*
— *face more honestly the reality of male privilege in society, and find ways to counter the violent and destructive aspects of our children's socialization.*
— *study carefully and teach creative, nonviolent ways to discipline our children.*

C. Violence in Leisure. Violence has long been part of leisure and entertainment, since the time of the first tragic dramas and publicly-staged fist fights. Modern society presents violence as entertainment through a bewildering variety of media, including books, magazines, comic books, movies, television, arcade games, video tapes, electronic games, personal computer games, music lyrics, and the Internet.

Dinner parties feature murder mysteries. Electronic games lead players to rape, eviscerate, and decapitate the enemy. Action hero toys and war game theaters cater to would-be warriors. Toys of violence give children practice in the actions and attitudes of violence. Professional sports often glorify violence and encourage winning at all costs.

News reports of violent acts have increased, despite declining rates of violent crime in North America. It appears that some editors have decided, "If it bleeds, it leads."

Violent content in entertainment has increased and become more explicit in the past decade. When violence is linked to sex in the entertainment media, it contributes to sexual violence and distorted ideas about sexuality and sexual pleasure. Studies suggest that violence in the media teaches children and adults to behave more violently, become desensitized to the harmful consequences of violence, and become more fearful of being attacked.[6]

Popular culture also perpetuates the myth that violence brings

---

6. Reported in the video *Beyond the News: TV Violence and Your Child* (Harrisonburg, Va.: Mennonite Media Ministries, 1996).

the victory of order over chaos, and that, if a "bad guy" commits violence against others, an indestructible "good guy" must use violence to vanquish such an irreformable "bad guy" and restore peace—until the next installment.

Jesus taught people to love their enemies, not exterminate them. Just as we guard ourselves and our loved ones against other dangers so, too, we must guard against the violence so prevalent in leisure today.

In response to violence in leisure, we call the church to:
— *advocate for and help create more choices in entertainment that are not based on violence.*
— *model cooperation, acceptance of differences, and nonviolent ways of resolving conflicts in our own lives.*
— *refrain from leisure activities that make a game of violence, or minimize the harmful consequences of violence.*
— *speak out against the "violence for profit" ethic that drives many of our leisure industries.*
— *screen our children's toys, games, television viewing, and play for violent content and intent.*
— *work to reduce violence in community and professional sports, and refuse to participate in such violence ourselves.*
— *watch newscasts with our children and teach them to be sensitive to other's pain.*
— *raise awareness to the desensitizing effects of using violent entertainment themes.*

D. Violence in Public Life. Violence in public life is tightly woven into the social fabric of North American society. Canada and the United States were established and much of their wealth obtained by the violent oppression and genocide of native peoples, the oppressive violence of slavery, and the exploitation of certain immigrant groups, women, and children for hard labor.

We confess that we have benefited from these atrocities. Much of the land that brought wealth to Mennonite families and congregations was available to our forebears because of this violence. Many of us, especially Mennonites of European background, have benefited and continue to benefit from white privilege, and from the economic and structural violence in society. Racism and other forms of deeply entrenched institutional injustice do violence to many in society, and continue to perpetuate and sanction the use of violence by one person or group against others.

Individualism and deteriorating family and social ties have been major factors in the recent growth of violence in North American public life. Many people no longer have the family and community connections that once served to control public violence.

Fear of violent attacks has grown. Many people, especially women, are afraid to go out alone at night. Public parks, streets, and parking facilities are perceived as dangerous, particularly after dark. Even church people are tempted to buy weapons for self-protection.

Weapons manufacturers advertise fingerprint-resistant handguns. The growth of gangs with ever more lethal weapons, illegal drug traffic, militia groups, bombings, and drive-by shootings has led to a demand for larger police forces, harsher penalties for crimes (including the death penalty), and more prisons.

Structures, systems, and institutions themselves are violent when they contribute to an atmosphere in which economic classes and ethnic groups are pitted against one another, and in which the antidote to violence is assumed to be more violence. High school youth are lured into expanded military cadet training that promotes violence as a solution to problems.

Violence does not overcome violence. As an alternative society within the broader society, the church can proclaim and demonstrate a different way. We can provide healing and hope by what we practice within the church, our workplaces, and neighborhoods. We can teach and demonstrate that biblical justice comes through peaceful means.

Many programs of healing and hope already exist within Mennonite circles and can serve as models for additional programs: victim-offender reconciliation programs, restorative justice programs, mediation networks, peace centers, prison ministries, peer mediation in schools, communication with legislators, and peace education programs. In addition, many congregations and individuals have created communities of love and accountability that counteract the violence in the surrounding society.

In response to violence in public life, we call the church at all levels to:

— *demonstrate a community of love and accountability within the church, call people into that community, and work to build community in neighborhoods and cities.*

— *work and pray in ways that confront the powers that promote institutional violence, racism, sexism, prejudice, and poverty.*

— *create and support programs of restorative justice, rather than punitive retribution, so that both offenders and victims can receive justice.*

— *establish friendships with people in prisons, demonstrating that no one, no matter what crime he or she has committed, is beyond the love of Christ.*

— *work to abolish capital punishment, wherever it has become law.*

— *advocate laws for greater restriction of the manufacture and possession of guns whose primary purpose is to kill or threaten human beings.*

— *teach and practice nonviolent conflict interventions and dispute mediation as third parties when others are involved in, or tempted to, violence.*

— *use the 1995 statement "Agreeing and Disagreeing in Love" as a guide to dealing with conflict in the church.*

— *teach the skills that enable people who are personally threatened with violence to act nonviolently, relying on love and creative responses rather than responding out of fear or using weapons for personal protection.*

— *develop programs within the church to train people in the spiritual disciplines of peace, nonviolence, forgiveness, loving enemies, and building relationships in the face of differences.*

E. Global Violence. Violence is also hurting the global community. Major armed conflicts continue in 40 countries. World military spending remains at U.S. $750 billion per year. Twenty-three thousand active nuclear weapons are still deployed, and 20 nations possess or are attempting to acquire nuclear weapons. One hundred million land mines have been sown around the world, and more are sown than removed each year. Over half the weapons sold to the Third World now come from the United States and Canada.[7] The threat of military violence continues to be used to manipulate and control other countries, and to enable wealthy countries to enlarge and protect their wealth at the expense of the world's poor. This vast economic and public policy commitment to violence presents a model of violent behavior that is imitated at all societal levels.

---

7. Project Ploughshares, *Armed Conflicts Report* (Waterloo, Ontario: Institute of Peace and Conflict Studies, 1996); Ruth L. Sivard, *World Military and Social Expenditures* (Washington, D.C.: World Priorities, 1996).

This armed violence is the result of nationalism, nations' unrestrained pursuit of self-interest, and the structural violence present in the world economic system. Ninety percent of the victims of this violence today are civilians, those who are weakest and least responsible for the economic disparity and the wars they must endure. Those who survive the violence are often disabled or made homeless or destitute by war. In nations no longer able to meet their citizens' basic needs, the resulting civil violence does lasting damage.

The victims of global violence are our brothers and sisters, made in the image of God. We affirm, as in previous statements,[8] that our first loyalty is to Jesus Christ and the kingdom of God, rather than to any earthly nation. We affirm our common humanity under God and our responsibility to care for the whole human family in the name of Jesus Christ.

In response to global violence, we call the church to:
- *restrain our own material desires and ambitions, and promote a fairer distribution of the world's resources, in order to reduce inequity, hunger, and hurt, which feed violence.*
- *identify the causal connections between socially-approved military and economic violence, and socially-disapproved personal and domestic violence.*
- *finance and pray for the work of our church agencies in promoting international justice, economic and personal well-being, respect for human rights, and participation in decision making.*
- *call on legislators to reduce military spending and arms sales, and to promote global justice.*
- *expand and publicize the range of nonviolent alternatives to conflict offered through our conciliation and mediation programs, and through direct interventions by Christian peacemakers.*
- *be steadfast in our refusal to participate in, train for, pay for, or directly profit from the use of military violence.*

---

8. "Peace and the Christian Witness," Mennonite Church, 1961; "A Christian Declaration on the Way of Peace," General Conference Mennonite Church," 1971; "Justice and the Christian Witness," Mennonite Church and General Conference Mennonite Church, 1983; "A Commitment to Christ's Way of Peace," Mennonite Central Committee, 1993; and "Confession of Faith in a Mennonite Perspective," General Conference Mennonite Church and Mennonite Church, 1995.

IV. Conclusion

The statement "Vision: Healing and Hope" calls us to "grow as communities of grace, joy, and peace so that God's healing and hope flow through us to the world." Therefore, we commit ourselves to **build church communities that demonstrate a peaceful alternative to violence** in all areas of our life together—communities that can serve as channels of God's healing and hope to a world angry and frightened by violence.

As members of the General Conference Mennonite Church and the Mennonite Church, with God's help, we commit ourselves, our congregations, and our church agencies to **be communities of nonviolence**, demonstrating and proclaiming the peaceful life to which Jesus Christ calls us. We commit ourselves to **teach nonviolence and peacemaking**, both within the church and beyond it. We choose to **confront, in the Spirit of Jesus Christ,** the powers, structures, institutions, and spirits of violence that tend to shape human behavior. We pledge our **love**, both to violence victims and to violence perpetrators. We will **encourage laws**, public institutions, and policies that work to reduce violence. We commit ourselves to **renounce the use of violence** and urge others to pledge the same.

> For I will leave in the midst of you
>   a people humble and lowly.
> They shall seek refuge in the name of the LORD—
>   the remnant of Israel;
> they shall do no wrong
>   and utter no lies,
> nor shall a deceitful tongue
>   be found in their mouths.
> Then they will pasture and lie down,
>   and no one shall make them afraid (Zeph. 3:12-13).

Prepared by the Joint Committee on Violence, appointed by the Mennonite Church General Board and the General Board of the General Conference Mennonite Church:
>   Lois Barrett, Wichita, Kansas
>   Florence Duley, Edmonton, Alberta
>   Doug Pritchard, Toronto, Ontario
>   Roger Steffy, Mechanicsburg, Pennsylvania

Adopted in principle by the delegates at the General Conference Mennonite Church Special Session in Winnipeg, Manitoba, July 8,

1997, and by the delegates at the Mennonite Church Assembly in Orlando, Florida, August 2, 1997.

Approved, as revised, by the General Boards on November 22, 1997, in Denver, Colorado.

Statement Summary

As Mennonites in Canada, the United States, and Puerto Rico, we have been affected by the violence which is pervasive in our world. While we affirm a commitment to peace and nonviolence, we have frequently tolerated and even benefited from some forms of violence. We have wrongly accepted, at least in part, the "myth of redemptive violence," the belief that good ends can come from violent means.

We define violence as **the human exercise of physical, emotional, social, or technological power which results in injury or harm to oneself or others**. Any form of human violence, whether mild or extreme, is an expression of evil.

One of the most basic issues in the Bible is how one deals with evil, and with violence in particular. The main direction of both the Old and New Testaments is toward nonviolence and reconciliation. We believe that God's love is greater than God's wrath. No violence committed against us, or those we love, justifies our committing violence in return. No suffering—not even death—can separate us from the love of God. The process of forgiveness is the way through suffering. When we choose the way of loving enemies, we are becoming transformed into Christ's image. All violence is fundamentally incompatible with the reign of Jesus Christ. Jesus calls us not to resist evil with violence—to forgive rather than to seek revenge—and to be peacemakers.

We experience violence in five ever-widening circles, from individual to global.

1. Violence may be directed against the self in various destructive behaviors. **We call the church** to counsel, nurture, and lead people away from all self-destructive behaviors. We also call the church to cherish and uphold the value of every human life.

2. We confess that, while we affirm a commitment to peace and nonviolence, many of us have allowed violence in our homes and churches. At the heart of nearly all violence in close relationships is the desire to control or use another person. We affirm the congregations and church agencies that have begun to respond to this form of violence. **We call the church** to move beyond denying and disbelieving domestic and professional abuse, and to make the church a safe place for abuse victims and survivors.

3. Violence has long been a part of leisure and entertainment. Violent content in entertainment is increasing, has become more explicit, and is often linked to sex. Society is becoming desensitized to the harmful consequences of violence. **We call the church** to advocate for and help create more choices in entertainment that are not based on violence.

4. Fear of violent attacks in public places has also grown. The increase in gangs and gun violence has led to a demand for larger police forces, more prisons, and harsher sentences. Structures and institutions are violent when economic classes, races, and ethnic groups are pitted against one another. As an alternative society, the church can proclaim and demonstrate a different way. Many programs of healing and hope already exist within Mennonite circles, and can serve as models. **We call the church** to create and support more programs of restorative justice and to teach the skills that enable people who are personally threatened with violence to respond nonviolently.

5. Violence is also hurting the global community. Major armed conflicts continue in nearly 40 countries. This armed violence is the result of nations' unrestrained pursuit of self-interest, and of the structural violence present in the world economic system. **We call the church** to restrain our own material desires and ambitions, and promote a fairer distribution of the world's resources. We also call the church to be steadfast in our refusal to participate in, train for, pay for, or directly profit from the use of military violence.

As members of the General Conference Mennonite Church and the Mennonite Church, with God's help, we commit ourselves, our congregations, and our church agencies to be communities of non-violence, demonstrating and proclaiming the life of peace to which Jesus Christ calls us.

Bibliography

1. Biblical and Theological Perspectives on Violence

Barrett, Lois. *The Way God Fights.* Scottdale, Pa.: Herald Press, 1987. Shows how God called the people of Israel away from violence to trust in the power of God to overcome evil.

Bonk, Jon. *The World at War, The Church at Peace.* Winnipeg, Man.: Kindred Press, 1988. Examines in a clear and concise way the Old and New Testament teachings on war and peacemaking.

Confession of Faith in a Mennonite Perspective. Scottdale, Pa.: Herald Press, 1995.

Narden, Terry. *The Ethics of War and Peace: Religious and Secular Perspectives.* Princeton, N. J.: Paul Christopher, 1996.

Wink, Walter. *Engaging the Powers.* Minneapolis: Augsburg Fortress Press, 1992. A wide-ranging study of the "myth of redemptive violence" through history and contemporary culture.

2. Violence Against Oneself

Lockley, John. *A Practical Workbook for the Depressed Christian.* 1991. A physician offers practical advice to sufferers, loved ones, and the church.

Mennonite Central Committee U.S. *Resource Packet on Abortion.* Akron, Pa., 1995. Provides facts on abortion, stories from various perspectives, church statements, and ways to respond.

Neufeld, Christine. *Peace—Just Live It! A Challenge to Youth for the 21st Century.* Newton, Kans.: Faith and Life Press, 1995. A 10-session curriculum for youth on peace broadly defined: peace with self, peace in close relationships, the media, economic justice, and political loyalties.

Shutt, Joyce M. *Steps to Hope: Coping with Dependency and Failure Through the Beatitudes and Twelve-Step Programs.* Scottdale, Pa.: Herald Press, 1990. Speaks to anyone trapped in destructive habits, pointing them back to our loving God.

3. Violence in Close Relationships

Beyond the News: Sexual Abuse (video). Harrisonburg, Va.: Mennonite Media Ministries, 1993. Intended for groups who wish to begin talking about sexual abuse.

Broken Vows: Religious Perspectives on Domestic Violence (video). Seattle: Center for the Prevention of Sexual and Domestic Violence, 1994.

Cooper-White, Pamela. *The Cry of Tamar: Violence Against Women and the Church's Response*. Minneapolis: Augsburg Fortress Press, 1995. Deals with power and its manifestation in sexual sins.

Fortune, Marie M. *Is Nothing Sacred? When Sex Invades the Pastoral Relationship*. San Francisco: Harper and Row, 1989. Examines the problem of clergy sexual misconduct against members of the congregation and suggests a model for responding to misconduct complaints.

_____. *Keeping the Faith: Guidance for Christian Women Facing Abuse*. San Francisco: Harper, 1987.

Heggen, Carolyn Holderread. *Sexual Abuse in Christian Homes and Churches*. Scottdale, Pa.: Herald Press, 1993. A resource for Christians who are willing to stop and listen to victims and perpetrators.

Mennonite Central Committee Domestic Violence Task Force. *The Purple Packet: Domestic Violence Resources for Pastoring Persons—Wife Abuse*. Akron, Pa., 1987. This and the following two resource packets raise awareness of the widespread domestic violence in church and society.

_____. *Broken Boundaries: Resources for Pastoring People—Child Sexual Abuse* (Blue Packet). 1989.

_____. *Crossing the Boundary: Sexual Abuse by Professionals* (Green Packet). 1991, 1993.

Miller, Melissa A. *Family Violence: The Compassionate Church Responds*. Scottdale, Pa.: Herald Press, 1994. Explores physical, sexual, and emotional abuse and the church's best response. Intended for group study.

Poling, James Newton. *The Abuse of Power*. Nashville: Abingdon, 1991. Deals with power and its manifestation in sexual sins.

Scott, Kay. *Sexual Assault: Will I Ever Feel Okay Again?* Minneapolis: Bethany House Publishers, 1993.

4. Violence and Leisure

Beyond the News: TV Violence and Your Child (video). Harrisonburg, Va.: Mennonite Media Ministries, 1996. This and the next video examine the effects of TV violence on the viewer and practical ways to counter it.

Beyond the News: TV Violence and You (video). Harrisonburg, Va.: Mennonite Media Ministries, 1996.

Fore, William. *Mythmakers: Gospel, Culture and the Media.* Cincinnati: Friendship Press, 1990. An expert on television and religion examines contemporary media.

Medved, Michael. *Hollywood vs. America: Popular Culture and the War on Traditional Values.* New York: Harper Collins, 1992. A film critic argues that the entertainment industry follows its own dark obsessions rather than the family-oriented material the public prefers.

5. Violence in Public Life

America's Original Sin: A Study Guide on White Racism. Washington, D.C.: Sojourners, n.d. This 180-page resource is divided into nine chapters. A leader's guide is available.

Beyond the News: Firearms Violence (video). Harrisonburg, Va.: Mennonite Media Ministries, 1994. Looks at causes of violence, effects, and the role Christians can play.

Beyond the News: Murder Close Up (video). Harrisonburg, Va.: Mennonite Media Ministries, 1994. Interviews with violence victims who describe their fear, anger, and forgiveness.

Beyond the News: Racism (video). Harrisonburg, Va.: Mennonite Media Ministries, 1993.

Free Indeed (video). Akron, Pa.: Mennonite Central Committee, 1995. 25 minutes. A drama in which four white, middle-class young adults play a card game as a prerequisite for doing a service project for a black Baptist church. The game leads to a discussion about the privileges of white people.

Grossman, Dave. *On Killing: The Psychological Cost of Learning To Kill in War and Society.* New York: Little, 1996.

Jackson, Dave. *Dial 911: Peaceful Christians and Urban Violence.* Scottdale, Pa.: Herald Press, 1981. Bare-to-the-soul stories and reflections about how Reba Place Fellowship has dealt with violence in Chicago.

Putting Down Stones; A Faithful Response to Urban Violence. Washington, D.C.: Sojourners, n.d. A four-session study for adults to help people set down their weapons and lay the foundation for peace-leading initiatives. A leader's guide is available.

Samuel, Dorothy T. *Safe Passage on City Streets.* Richmond, Ind.: Liberty Literary Works, 1991. Describes nonviolent ways to decrease your chances of being attacked, reduce your fears, and increase your chances of surviving any attack.

Shearer, Jody Miller. *Enter the River: Healing Steps from White Privilege Toward Racial Reconciliation*. Scottdale, Pa.: Herald Press, 1994. Presents basic ideas on the role of church and societal racism.

Yoder, John H. *What Would You Do?* Scottdale, Pa.: Herald Press, 1983. Outlines and comments on the possible responses to violence; includes stories where nonviolence worked.

6. Global Violence

Beyond the News: Hope for Bosnia (video). Harrisonburg, Va.: Mennonite Media Ministries, 1993. Interviews with inspiring Christians doing Christ's peacemaking work in the midst of war.

Curle, Adam. *Another Way: Positive Response to Contemporary Violence*. Oxford, U.K.: Jon Carpenter, 1995. Shows that, in the worst of contemporary violence, love is the only response that works.

Decide for Peace. Canadian and U.S. packets on choosing whether to be a conscientious objector to war. Available from the Commission on Home Ministries, P.O. Box 347, Newton, Kansas 67114. Includes the book *Decide for Peace* by Eddy Hall (Newton, Kans.: Faith and Life Press, 1996).

Hostetler, Marian. *They Loved Their Enemies*. Scottdale, Pa.: Herald Press, 1988. Stories from Africa of Christians who forgave their enemies even in the face of violence.

Lederach, John Paul. *Preparing for Peace: Conflict Transformation Across Cultures*. Syracuse, N.Y.: Syracuse University Press, 1996. Portrays Mennonite thinking on conflict resolution across cultures. Anecdotal, reflecting the author's many experiences.

McManus, Philip, and Schlabach, Gerald. *Relentless Persistence: Nonviolent Action in Latin America*. Philadelphia: New Society Publishers, 1990. Testimonies and reflections on efforts at nonviolent social change through people's movements.

Peachey, Titus, and Peachey, Linda Gehman. *Seeking Peace*. Intercourse, Pa.: Good Books, 1991. True stories of Mennonites around the world, struggling to live their belief in peace. Full of courage and spirit.

Ruth-Heffelbower, Duane. *The Anabaptists Are Back!* Herald Press, 1991. Argues from theology and experience that nonviolent confrontation is the essence of our original Anabaptist nonresistance. Includes many dramatic testimonies.

Sider, Ronald J. *Nonviolence: The Invincible Weapon?* Waco, Tex.: Word Publishing, 1989. Tells the story of the nonviolent revolutions from ancient times to the Philippines in the 1980s.

Stories

Whose Responsibility?

When I first saw the Power Rangers show, I was shocked to see the large amount of violence. I purposely tuned into the show the following day to see if this level of violence was a daily occurrence. I was appalled to see a "viewer discretion" warning before this particular episode. A warning before a children's show pushed my tolerance to the limit. This was the extreme of irresponsible TV.

Putting my anger in motion, I sent a letter along with a petition to the television station that was airing the Power Rangers. Having received no reply after a month, I called and was told that it would continue to be aired as it was one of the top three shows and "the children wanted it."

I was unimpressed with this reply, so I lodged a formal complaint to the Canadian Radio and Television Commission (CRTC). They, in turn, forwarded my complaint to the Canadian Broadcasting Standards Council, who told the television station they must respond to my letter. They did, only to say they considered the show action-oriented and not violent, and would continue to broadcast Power Rangers.

Over the next few months, the CRTC received a number of other complaints concerning this show. A few broadcasters pulled the show, but not the station to which I complained. They were given the option of either pulling the show, or having the Los Angeles producers of the show modify it to conform with the Canadian Codes. They did, in fact, meet with the producers of the show, and as of now, the show is still being aired in a minimally modified form. The victory is a small one: the show has been modified and now includes public service announcements about dealing positively with conflict, not smoking, etc. I feel that these positive messages are overpowered by the negative messages, and that this show is unsuitable for children. The amount and high level of violence is unacceptable; it is still portrayed as a method of overcoming conflict. All the fighting action moves are still present to be imitated by children, and all of the weapons are still being used. It still gives unhealthy messages: lack of respect for property, and for human beings. I do not see the value of this show and others like it.

Small children like to act out what they see. And when they act out these violent scenes—kick-boxing and punching—they discover that they get hurt and even bleed, something they didn't see on TV.

My main concern is to create a more positive future. This goes far beyond the battle of the Mighty Morphin' Power Rangers. It is a plea for all concerned citizens to speak out against media violence and encourage shows that promote more positive behaviour. It is the responsibility of every adult to demand more of the television industry in order to create a more wholesome society for children. They are our future.

—excerpts from "Controlling TV Violence: Whose Responsibility?" a pamphlet written by Kathryn Flannery for Peace Factory, 1995. Used with permission.

Threatened at Gunpoint

Linda and I were walking from our home on Adams to the parsonage to offer our condolences to Joan Gerig, who had just been told that her mother had died that morning in Iowa. We walk to church all the time, and just that morning had walked all around Garfield Park on our semi-regular 6:15 a.m., two-mile, in-the-dark outing with Joan and two older neighborhood ladies. So we didn't think anything about walking to the church at 8 a.m. But we made a big mistake when we took the shortcut past the liquor store on Fifth, then through the alley.

We crossed Van Buren and kept going down the alley toward Congress. About two-thirds of the way down, I spotted a roofing nail lying on the street and, following my habit of preventing as many flat tires as possible, I bent down and picked it up. When I straightened back up, there was a guy standing right in front of me. I smiled, showed him the nail and said, "Just saved another $5."

He pointed his pistol at me, then said through a ski mask, "Give me your money."

The only thing I could think to say was, "Man, I'm sorry. I don't have any money on me. But we work for that church over there, and if you'll come with us to the church, we'll see if we can find something for you."

He waved his pistol at me and shouted something about giving him the money or he would shoot.

I told him I didn't have any money, but if he'd just follow us maybe we could find some for him. Then Linda, in an irritated tone of voice, said, "We're going to visit a woman whose mother just passed away." And we both turned and went down the narrow path between the backyard fences and the day care playground fence. I waved for him to follow us and said, "Come on." Halfway down the path, I turned to see if he was following, but he was just standing there in the alley looking at us. When we got to the back entrance to the church, which is also Joan's backyard, Linda went up the stairs that lead to the upper church door, and I knocked on

Joan's back door. When she opened it, I turned and saw [the man] running back across Van Buren heading north.

Almost everyone we have told about the incident has been horrified at how we responded, and has given us advice on how to be "better victims." I will admit that, although at the moment I was not aware of any fear or panic, I did think when I turned and walked away that I was about to get shot in the back.

Looking back on it, we realize that a couple of things have changed for us in a negative sense. One thing is that we have become more careful when we are out, looking both ways when we leave the house or get out of the car. And we are now sure that we want to keep the car here in a city with great public transportation. Speaking of which, we will probably use the el a little less, especially if we have to wait for a train after dark or get off at a deserted station. That makes me angry, as well.

—written by Lynn Miller, first published in The Mennonite, February 13, 1996. Used with permission.

Time for Healing

It is easy to believe that violence will never touch our lives in a personal way. For me, this notion was shattered, along with some of my understandings of God, on the evening of June21, 1994, when I was abducted from my home at knifepoint, threatened repeatedly, and raped in a motel room. In the end, my assailant became more agitated, and I felt I must take a chance at escaping or be killed. In my attempt to escape, he caught me, and I had to struggle against the knife, cutting my hand severely. I did, however, manage to get out and ran to the motel office where I received help. He escaped, but then later turned himself in, pled guilty, and was sentenced for his crimes.

We knew this man—or thought we did. Never did I suspect the events of that evening would unfold as they did when I opened the door and let this man into my home. I was under the impression he had come to our home to seek advice and counsel about his failing marriage from my husband, who was in the back room with our two-year-old daughter, and was threatened and warned not to call the police. My husband was the pastor of the small church which this man attended irregularly. He had been to our home twice that day (while I was at work) and spoke to my husband about his problems. What started out as something we considered a ministry turned out to be the most terrifying and violence-filled event of our lives.

Needless to say, this caused us to ask many hard questions, such as, "Why would God allow this tragedy when we were there to do God's work?" We received a variety of comments and suggestions from well-meaning Christians who seemed to feel the need to provide "answers" to fill in the blanks, and explain away the mysteries surrounding God and God's role in this trauma. Some of the least helpful and perhaps the most hurtful comments suggested and implied that this event had actually been orchestrated by God in order to fulfill some divine purpose or bring about growth in our lives. Many people said, "God has a purpose for this." I did not want to believe that the God I had loved and served and trusted for many years would *cause* such a traumatic event for my greater good or growth.

The more helpful and healing comments did not attempt to provide "answers" or explanations, but simply reminded us that there exists sin and evil in this world—only God knows why things are allowed to happen as they do—but a loving and compassionate God would not cause his children to suffer in order to bring about a specific end. God weeps *with* us, and while God does not *cause* these sufferings for some purpose, he *can* and *does* bring good out of brokenness.

We encountered another unhelpful look at the problem of suffering in a book given to us by a relative. The author of this book, who had been abused as a child, suggested that we, who are but sinners and guilty of causing Christ's suffering, deserve nothing less than what we get. Perhaps there were good points in this book as well, but I was blinded by this absurd way of explaining the problem of suffering.

Another very hurtful response came from the denominational church leadership. We felt very much as if they trivialized our experience and the trauma and brokenness it brought to our lives. They heard our story and seemed sympathetic, but then suggested right away that we could perhaps return to our church or simply pastor another church, as if we could just go on without taking time for healing. We felt rushed. We got the impression from these people and others that they were concerned that, if we got out of the ministry scene for awhile, we might never get back into it. But right then it was the last thing we wanted or had energy to do. We needed and desired time for healing—time to be *ministered to*. We simply were unable to be in a position of ministry at that point, but many did not comprehend this. In a way, we felt abandoned by them.

Some people also trivialized our experience by relating stories of similar experiences in which victims prayed and witnessed to their attackers, turning the situation around and even leading their attackers to Christ. Those were nice stories, but they implied that, if we had had enough faith, prayed hard enough, or said the right things, perhaps I would not have been raped or my attacker would have had a life-changing encounter with God. I'm afraid it just did not happen that way, despite the fact that I prayed almost constantly during the ordeal!

After the church my husband had been pastoring decided to close, we resettled in a new home and began to pick up the pieces. We longed desperately to find a church home where we could share our story and find healing. It was a long time before we found such a

place. The churches we tried seemed busy, caught up, and not ready
or able to share and bear the pain of newcomers. It felt like a game—
getting dressed up, going to church, and coming home, never really
scratching the surface of our pain. We were unable to penetrate su-
perficial relationships and worship experiences. We needed to experience the church, and were beginning to give up hope of ever coming
among friends in faith and worship.

Then we found our present church. The first Sunday we attended, we felt an atmosphere of true healing and wholeness. *This*
was a place we could share our story. *These* were people who would
hear our story, share our pain, help us bear the load, and minister to
us in a healing way. The *atmosphere* of openness and healing, more
than any spoken words, drew us back again, and our first impres-
sions were correct. We have had the opportunity to share our story
with a number of people, and we have found abundant healing in
telling the story to sensitive, open-minded people who have been
quick to listen, cry with us, and hug, and slow to provide quick or pat
answers. The continual focus on healing and wholeness we have felt
has brought us leaps and bounds beyond where we imagined we'd
be. Because we have experienced healing, we have, in turn, been able
to minister healing to others who are hurting.

—*written by Patty and Roy Stetler, Dillsburg, Pennsylvania*

Parents of Slain Prisoner Plead for Mercy for Their Son's Killer

The scene was a Philadelphia courtroom. On June 12, a young prisoner named David was to receive his sentence for murdering another prisoner at Holmesburg, Philadelphia's county prison.

The district attorney, out for a maximum sentence to enhance
his reputation, elaborated on the stab wounds. He paused before
the victim's parents, mother Theresa and stepfather Conrad Moore,
so that attention would be drawn to their tears. That morning, he
had told the parents of slain prisoner Gerald Anderson that they
would have a chance to speak if they wished.

"We're not stupid," Theresa said. "We knew we were being
manipulated. He wanted us to cry. He wanted us to say 'Hang 'im,
bone 'im, skin 'im alive! (*The Hobbit*).' But I thanked God for the
opportunity to speak. I prayed so hard as I waited, 'Jesus, help me!'
I prayed that I wouldn't get hysterical, that I could just say what I
need to say."

The judge leaned back in her chair, getting sleepy. Most of the
sentences she handed out were determined in advance, but the victim's family impact statements were often therapeutic for them,
and she prepared for the standard speeches of grief by distancing
herself.

"You want to know the impact of Gerald's death?" Theresa
asked. "Our only son is dead. His children no longer have a father.
You can't have more impact than that. I will miss my son every day
for the rest of my life.

"But I have forgiven David. I don't want Gerald's killer to
spend his life in jail. The death penalty isn't going to bring my son
back. It would give me no satisfaction whatsoever to know he will
be in jail the rest of his life.

"I'm a Christian; I believe in God. And I have to believe that
God doesn't allow anything to happen outside his control. I need
to trust in him. Every day I think about how God is forgiving me. It
hurt God when they hurt his son. But he was showing us that it is
all about forgiveness.

"And if I, Gerald's mother, can forgive David, then the court should be able to be lenient."

By now, the judge was leaning forward, her mouth ajar. There was dead silence in the courtroom.

Conrad, too, gave a statement, also expressing his forgiveness for the terrible act. "Even though he murdered Gerald," says Conrad, "all he has to do is ask God for forgiveness, and God will freely grant it. Knowing that, who are we to withhold forgiveness?!"

"I have never seen anything like this," the judge responded. "I have never seen grace and mercy exemplified like this."

The sentence handed down, however, was 20 years on top of the original 20 years the young man was serving, so he will spend most of his adult life in prison.

After the sentencing, the Moores hugged David's weeping family, and there was love, support, and forgiveness expressed. The families forgot that the court was still in session, and no one interrupted the drama to tell them to "take it outside."

David asked to speak to the Moores personally after the trial; he was able to express how sorry he was. He also tried to comfort them, and told them that he and others on the street had known that Gerald was innocent of the murder charge that had sent him to prison. Conrad invited him to write to them, promising that he would return a letter and support him as he could. "He needs to see God's grace and forgiveness shown through people, especially now," Conrad said.

"The judge and the lawyers, they have their jobs to do," Theresa said. "But sentencing? That isn't my job. As a Christian my job is to reveal Christ."

Justice System Gives Parents Fuel for Anger in Painful Process

A year and a half after Gerald Anderson's murder, his parents were grateful for the sense of closure that his killer's trial and sentencing produced. They were able to forgive the man face to face and put much of the pain behind them. But was it easy? No. The process has been excruciating, they say. Here are a few pictures of the process through which they moved.

"So much fuel for bitterness, so much fuel . . ." Conrad says.

Within days after they were notified of their son's murder in Holmesburg, Conrad and Theresa Moore arrived at the prison to claim his belongings. They were still in shock, still hoping the news wasn't true. They hoped to find some of Gerald's keepsakes for his three children and themselves, as though his Bible, books, jacket, or pajamas might contain something tangible of the fun-loving, free-spirited, and likable young man they loved.

The assistant warden was reluctant to tear himself away from his newspaper; he made them wait. His first comment was not an apology for the terrible tragedy; it was a cold statement. "You can't have Gerald's money unless you brought a copy of the death certificate."

What money? Theresa thought. The only money he had was what Conrad and I sent him from time to time. He had $32. Does he think I'm here for my son's money?

The man returned with a sack full of Gerald's belongings, which he tossed on the counter "like someone putting out the trash." Finally, the warden came out. He, too, bypassed any word of condolence or apology for the 26-year-old trustee's stabbing death. He simply noted that, since there were legal matters pending, he was unable to talk to them about the incident.

Would it have impeded the legal process to express a kind word to us in our grief? Conrad wondered. "The level of insensitivity was monumental at that prison," Conrad said. "I found myself wondering how any person in the world could get through this experience without Christ."

Shortly after Gerald's death, his mother Theresa was contacted by a Grief Assistance Program caseworker. She encouraged Theresa to file an application for some compensation from Pennsylvania's Crime Victims' Compensation Board, money that could have been used to cover the funeral expenses. Months later, a form letter arrived from the board. Again, there was not one personal word about their loss. Instead, the letter coldly denied their compensation claim. "The Crime Victims' Compensation Act was created to assist innocent victims of crime. . . . Any individual . . . killed while incarcerated . . . cannot be considered an innocent victim," the letter stated.

The letter was particularly ironic in light of the fact that Gerald's life sentence for murder had been overturned. He was awaiting a retrial because the chief witness admitted in court that she had lied in identifying Gerald.

"Bitterness, anger, grieving . . . the letter reopened all the wounds for us," Conrad said. "There was no justice, no fairness for us in the legal system. The tragedy kept compounding."

Denial, bargaining ("please, let it be someone else dead; let it all be a misunderstanding, and I will . . ."), anger, depression, acceptance, forgiveness—these are the stages both Theresa and Conrad lived through.

The night they got the news of Gerald's death, Conrad prayed, "God, I am positively not adequate, not equipped to be what Theresa needs me to be in this. Please be to her what I can't be."

Months later, Theresa found herself spending all her spare time aside from church and work on the sofa in front of the TV. One day, it dawned on her that her listlessness was depression, and she and Conrad together went to see a counselor. "I took Prozac for a few months until I began to feel better, and the counseling helped. In all this, Conrad never complained, although I found out later how worried he was about me. I have seen my husband become more like Christ through this year.

"We decided very early on that we would need to forgive Gerald's killer. Forgiveness was a fact, but we didn't really feel it until we said it in the courtroom. We prayed that God would enable us to forgive, and not to hate. God will give us the desires of our heart, but we have to want it.

"Some people believe that getting revenge, or even justice, will heal their grief. But that is misplaced hope. We didn't want to be victims, too. Are we going to be like those families who go to the parole hearing each year to protest and make sure the prisoner remains in jail—opening those wounds year after year? Somehow, people think that their loved one won't rest in peace unless the individual who did the crime is punished. But that ain't it!

"We watched two people very carefully. Ronald Goldman's father (O.J. Simpson trial) seems, to us, to have gone from a grieving father to an angry, hostile person looking for revenge in an unjust trial and legal system. His face has changed. He seems to have become a victim along with his murdered son. Sharon Tate's mother (Charles Manson trial), on the other hand, began a program working with inmates after her daughter's vicious murder, and her work has produced untold good in people's lives.

"It was obvious to us from the beginning that we had the same choices to make. We could become bitter, angry, and hostile, and shrivel up, or we could ask God to come in and redeem the situation.

"After we had expressed forgiveness in the courtroom, we realized it was the first time we were able to take charge and wield some power by doing what only we could do. Ever since then, we have had such peace. It felt like drowning, then coming up for air. Breathing feels so good, so natural. Forgiveness gave us that release. This is what we are supposed to be, what God wants us to be.

"The most healing thing for us has been to be connected to Word of Joy (Creamery, Pennsylvania), a church community that has comforted and loved us through all this. God always used someone to bring comfort through a note, a word, a hug, a book. Through them, God let us know that he was angry, too, that he was watching, and was with us. Gerald had accepted Christ as his Savior. He freely spoke about his faith with others. That also gives us peace. We know he is free; free at last, with the Lord."

—*written by Mary Lou Cummings for the Franconia Conference News, September 1996. Conrad Moore is director of Liberty House, a residence and mentoring program for newly-released Christian prisoners, Schwenksville, Pennsylvania. Theresa Moore works at Wampler Longacre Company.*

Neighborhood Closes Second Crack House

On March 5, 1996, Columbia Heights residents in Washington, D.C., and Christian Peacemaker Team members stood in front of the boarded-up crack house at 2719 13th Street N.W. with candles and signs to celebrate the neighborhood's victory. Years of citizen action and a recent intensive campaign of letters and phone calls about violence and illegal activity prompted city authorities to close the building for housing violations. Rush hour traffic came to a halt as motorists stopped to watch the festivities that had replaced the more common sight of drug dealing and prostitution. Neighbors continued to join the group as the news spread that the house had indeed been closed.

Paul Dahmus, a neighborhood resident, had been concerned about the poor conditions of the house for 10 years. Dahmus remembers the landlord, Russell Hughes, for the 1988 fire at one of his properties in which three small children were burned to death. "We know that the community has to keep pressure on these dangerous neighborhood places. We are learning how to make things happen. I'm pleased to add this second neighborhood nuisance to our list of closings. We expect the list to continue to grow," Dahmus says. Hughes has been working to correct the housing violations and promises to make a concerted effort to sell the house as a single-family unit.

In December 1994, a similar problem house was closed just two blocks from 2719 13th Street N.W. The owner of that house, Kingsley Anyanwataku, is now serving a six-year jail sentence for housing violations and tax evasion. Anyanwataku owned a string of more than 40 drug houses in the District.

—written by Tammy Krause for Christian Peacemaker Team Sunday packet, October 1996

Prayers on the Rooftop

On February 28, 1996, Christian Peacemaker Team members were alerted that the destruction of several homes in and around Hebron was imminent. As team members hurried to the reported area, they came across a family quickly collecting their belongings into haphazard piles. The Zaloum family had lived in their home for the last three years in the shadow of one of the largest settlements in the West Bank on property they had owned for generations. There was already a bulldozer parked in their yard. While the military claimed they had given the family 24-hours notice to vacate the premises, the family said they were alerted only when soldiers arrived and started throwing all their possessions out into the yard.

As Israeli soldiers ringed the house, yelling and beating Palestinians to make them leave, four CPTers climbed onto the rooftop of the house to sing and pray, and attempt to stop the pending demolition. Then the bulldozer was fired up, and soldiers climbed up to the roof to drag the CPTers away. Team members Dianne Roe, 53, Corning, New York, and Robert Naiman, 30, Urbana, Illinois, were arrested and spent 48 hours in jail.

CPTer Cole Hull, Seattle, Washington, succeeded in contacting a member of the Knesset (Israeli parliament), who took the matter to then-Prime Minister Shimon Perez. A desist order was issued, but it came moments too late to save the Zaloum family home. The house was reduced to rubble, leaving 15 people homeless. The family wept beside the ruins while the soldiers laughed and joked. Some soldiers said the home was destroyed in reprisal for the February 25 bus bombings in Jerusalem and Ashkelon.

Though CPT's efforts could not stop the destruction of the Zaloums' home, the desist order stood, and six other houses slated for demolition were spared that day. CPTers' act of prayer and resistance on the rooftop had delayed the military long enough to make a difference. Subsequent international pressure and heightened publicity further delayed the forced removal of families from their homes and properties in the area.

After their release from jail, Roe and Naiman were held under house arrest in Hebron until their scheduled deportation hearing on March 4. When the police failed to appear at that hearing, the deportation process was delayed indefinitely, but the charges can apparently be pursued at any time. CPT director Gene Stoltzfus said, "I am sure that the torrent of faxes, e-mail, and phone calls from the United States played a big role in the government's decision not to pursue the case, at least for the moment."

—*written by Cole Hull for Christian Peacemaker Team Sunday packet, October 1996*

A Mennonite Statement on Violence

Study Guide

by Lois Barrett

This guide is best used in adult study groups, where shared experiences and community action can sharpen the learning. We assume that each participant will have a copy of the statement and study guide, and will be prepared to reflect and act on the material between sessions.

Session 1   A Biblical and Theological Overview
Session 2   Violence Against Self and Violence in Close Relationships
Session 3   Violence in Leisure and Violence in Society
Session 4   Global Violence
Session 5   Discipling Toward Nonviolence
Session 6   Next Steps

Each of the six sessions are structured in the following sequence:

a) **Reflect on your experience**—through personal storytelling and discussion of stories appended to the statement (pages 24-38)

b) **Think biblically**—through reading and discussing selected Scripture passages.

c) **Plan possibilities**—through discerning possible outcomes of learning.

d) **Act on it**—by testing out the learnings either in the session or between sessions. (Sessions two to six begin by reflecting on action from the previous session)

Lois Barrett is executive secretary of the Commission on Home Ministries of the General Conference Mennonite Church. She is a member of the Mennonite Church of the Servant in Wichita, Kansas.

Suggestions for those leading the study:

- Survey the whole study at the outset, and plan which books or other resources you would like to use from the Going deeper sections or the bibliography on page 19.

- Some sessions could be stretched into two (particularly sessions 2 and 3). If you have extra session time available, feel free to plan further sessions.

- Read the session questions and Scripture passages thoroughly before each session.

- Be aware that there are plenty of questions for discussion. Plan ahead which themes and questions are most important to your group, and which ones you'll have time for.

- Structure the sessions to be more than head exercises. Make sure you probe personal application and experience.

- Incorporate worship at the beginning and/or end of the sessions.

Session 1
Violence—A Biblical and Theological Overview

Reflect on your experience

North Americans are concerned about violence. Newspaper stories and television broadcasts seem to be filled with it. Many are afraid, especially of the possibility of violent crime by strangers. At the same time, much of the violence in North American society includes acts committed among people in close relationships. It also includes subtle kinds of violence that do not make the news.

This study, based on the document "And No One Shall Make Them Afraid: A Mennonite Statement on Violence," attempts to look broadly at human violence in our society from individual violence to the massive violence of war.

However, there are some kinds of violence the statement does not cover. The scope of this study does not include violence against the environment—pollution, destruction of forests, extinction of animal species—or the "violence" of the environment—such as tornadoes, hurricanes, avalanches, volcanos, poisonous plants and animals, and disease-bearing organisms.

Nor does this study discuss the so-called violence of God, known in the Bible as the wrath of God. However we may try to explain the past, present, or eventual destruction of enemies or evildoers, we know from the New Testament and especially from Jesus that God's main characteristic is love. This is the aspect of God that we are called to imitate. Jesus asks us to be like God in loving enemies (Luke 6:32-36; Matt. 5:43-48).

Instead of trying to penetrate the mysteries of God's action, our study sessions will focus on an area where the New Testament is extremely clear: *our* action. This study is about violence as the "human exercise of physical, emotional, social, or technological power which results in injury or harm to oneself or others." This is violence we can do something about.

Just as there are kinds of violence, there are also *degrees* of violence. At one end of the spectrum are verbal threats, emotional abuse, and intimidation, which may do emotional harm. At the other end are physically damaging or lethal acts such as murder, beatings, shootings, rape, and sexual abuse, as well as organized mass violence like war.

Share in the Group: What are your fears, worries, and concerns about violence? How has violence affected you? Physically? Emotionally? Spiritually? How have you or those close to you experienced violence?

Think biblically

Read Section II of the statement, "Biblical and Theological Foundations." In broad strokes, retell biblical history related to violence and peacemaking, from creation to the age to come. (Note that even in Old Testament stories of wars, God restricted human violence and saved people from enemies in surprising ways, beyond any human efforts.)

Read and discuss **John 18:33-37**. What is the nature of Jesus' kingdom? In contrast to that of most governments, what is the defense policy of the reign of God?

Read and discuss Romans 12:1-21. What do verses 1 and 2 say about conforming to the way the world usually does things? What should a Christian do instead? In the following verses, what do you find that echoes Jesus' teaching on violence? Under what circumstances does this passage suggest that it is all right for Christians to practice violence or take revenge? Compare this passage with Leviticus 19:18. What do both texts suggest we do when someone else acts with evil intent toward us?

On newsprint or chalkboard, make two lists: (1) What does Romans tell us *not* to do with regard to violence? (2) What positive actions does Romans call us to do? Note that, if violence is evil, then when we try to combat evil with violence, we, too, are acting in an evil way, and are overcome by evil. What is the only way to stop the cycle of violence?

Comment: If his were a kingdom like Pilate's or Caesar's, Jesus might have asked his followers to take up arms to keep him from being arrested and killed. They would have used violence to combat violence. Peter, in fact, tried to do just that, but Jesus told him to put his sword back into its sheath (John 18:10-11). Jesus let himself be arrested, ill-treated, and crucified rather than fight back with violence. More than that, he asked his disciples to "follow me." That is, he asked them to follow him in his life, his teachings, and his death, in the hope of also following him in resurrection.

Jesus' followers are not to use violence, even when violence is committed against them. Menno Simons, early Anabaptist leader in the low countries, wrote:

> Christ did not want to be defended with Peter's sword. How can a Christian then defend himself with it? Christ wanted to drink the cup which the Father had given him; how then can a Christian avoid it?[1]

Plan possibilities

The "Biblical and Theological Foundations" section of the statement lists five theological understandings about violence (page 4). Depending on your time available, choose from the following options in exploring how these understandings may be put into practice. You may want to divide into smaller groups.

1. Often when someone is killed, you may hear it said, "It was the will of God," or "God took her." The assumption behind statements like these is that everything that happens is the will of God, or that God and humans are the only actors in the world. This completely ignores the presence of evil forces, which often go beyond individual human sins. Sometimes, in this age, evil keeps God's will from being done. Discuss: If a child were kidnapped and killed, how would you respond to someone who told the parents, "This was the will of God"? How would you explain what God is like?

2. For children, and sometimes adults, "He hit me first" becomes a justification for further violence. Imagine yourself arbitrating in

---

1. "The Blasphemy of John of Leiden," in *The Complete Writings of Menno Simons*, ed. by Leonard Verduin and J. C. Wenger (Scottdale, Pa.: Herald Press, 1956), 45.

such a situation of conflict. Rooting your response in the way of Jesus, list as many creative, nonviolent responses as possible for the one on the receiving end of the "hitting".

3. With the threat of violence often comes fear. List as many forms as violence as you can, and name the fears that come with each. Then brainstorm how we as Christians can confront those fears. What can we do to keep reminding ourselves and each other that "nothing can separate us from the love of God"? Share your responses in the larger group.

4. When we do not forgive, our anger and hate eat away at us from the inside and threaten to destroy us. We are called to forgive, even though the other person does not repent. This does not mean that the other person should not suffer consequences of his or her offense and lack of repentance. It also does not mean that forgiveness happens instantaneously or easily. It is also to be distinguished from the "binding and loosing" ministry of the church (Matthew 18:18). Discuss: What resources does your congregation provide for people working through a forgiveness process? How can we help each other move through the stages of forgiveness—denial, anger, depression, bargaining, and acceptance? Some congregations have times of confession in the worship service. What other elements in a worship service might be helpful? You may want to write a litany or design a part of a worship service focusing on healing and forgiving.

5. The Christian life is to be one of transforming into the image of Christ, who is himself the image of God. Transformation implies a process of becoming more and more like Christ. Share your points of transformation on the issue of loving enemies. What transformation are you still hoping for? How might you share this with someone who is not a Christian, or with a Christian who takes a different position on loving enemies?

Act on it

Write down incidents of violence that you experience, hear or read about between now and the next session. Also note others' responses (or yours) to that violence. In these situations, what would it have meant for one or more key people not to conform to the pattern of this world, but to be transformed to act like Jesus? Bring your notes to the next session.

If members of the group have experienced violence in their own lives that still needs to be healed or forgiven, it may be helpful to schedule a service of healing and prayer or sessions of pastoral counseling. Check privately with those affected and with your pastor concerning what is appropriate.

For next time:
Read Sections III.A. and III.B. of the Statement on Violence.

Going deeper

Those who want to go deeper into the biblical and theological understandings of violence will want to study some of the books listed in the bibliography (page 19).

The Way God Fights is a simply written book on the question of holy war in the Old Testament. Did God approve of violence?

Engaging the Powers (together with Walter Wink's earlier books on the "principalities and powers") is a comprehensive study of the domination system, as Wink calls the world's system built on violence. Worth the price of the book is the chapter "On Not Becoming What We Hate." There is also a study of Daniel in relation to the question of why God doesn't always answer our prayers right away.

Article 22 of *Confession of Faith in a Mennonite Perspective* is on "Peace, Justice, and Nonresistance." A deeper study of the entire confession will reveal how the theme of peace is woven throughout.

Session 2

Violence Against Self and Violence in Close Relationships

Reflect on your experience

Share: Incidents of violence you recorded since the last session. Reflect on how Christians have responded or might respond. Then:

Option 1
Read and discuss the story, "Time for Healing" (page 28). What made this experience so traumatic? How did Patty and Roy experience the responses of the church? What helped healing?

Option 2
Share: If you know people who have attempted suicide or committed suicide, or those who have done violence against themselves in some other way (drugs, for example), reflect on the trauma of the events. In what ways did the church respond?

Think biblically

Review: From your reading of sections III A and III B of the violence statement, review the range of behaviors that are included in violence against oneself and violence in close relationships. List them on a sheet of newsprint or on the chalkboard.

Note that abortion is included in both categories, as violence against the woman and violence against the fetus. No matter what your position is on abortion, or whether you think the fetus is a human being or simply part of the woman's body, abortion is still violent in nature.

Read and discuss 2 Corinthians 5:19-20. What does the text say about the value of the body? For Christians, to whom does their body belong? Should Christians make decisions about their bodies without checking it out with God? What is the body to be used for?

Read and discuss Matthew 5:21-24 and Colossians 3:5-17. What do's and don'ts for close relationships can we find in these passages? Make two lists: characteristics of the "old self" and characteristics of the "new self", which is "being renewed . . . according to the image of its Creator." How does the new self relate to people close at hand, to family, to others in the church? How does Jesus go beyond "do not murder" in close relationships?

What does it mean for two people in a close relationship to be reconciled, when one has abused the other in some way, especially when physical violence has been used? In the Matthew passage, which party has the greatest responsibility for reconciliation and changed behavior—the one who has committed the offense, or the one against whom the offense was committed? What encourages or prevents such reconciliation in your church?

How might the "rules" of Colossians 3:5-17 apply to those who are in a power position and to those with less power? What would it mean for those with more power to clothe themselves with compassion, kindness, humility, meekness, patience, forgiveness, and love?

Option for further discussion:

Colossians 3:18-4:1 applies the foregoing teaching to people in various relationships of unequal power: wives and husbands, children and fathers, slaves and masters. Note that in each case the persons assumed to have less power are addressed first and treated as people capable of acting morally. Then note the instructions for husbands, fathers, and masters.

How are these instructions in keeping with the teaching earlier in the chapter? What would it mean for people with power to act in accordance with Paul's teaching here? Does Paul think that those with power should be held less accountable for following Jesus?

Think of times in your life when you have been powerful, or powerless. How do Paul's words in Colossians 3:5-4:1 apply to both situations?

Comment: The body is sacred.

In the first century, many philosophers in the Greek-Roman world thought that only the soul really counted and the body was unimportant. In contrast, the early church developed theological statements about Jesus being completely divine *and* completely human. The letter of 1 John emphasizes that Jesus came *in the flesh*. For Christians the body was not to be ignored. Most of the church (ex-

cept for a group known as gnostics) reflected the Hebrew under-
standing that it wasn't possible for you to sin in your body without
any effect on the soul. Soul, mind, and body were a unity. For
Jesus, the great commandment is to love God with heart, soul,
mind, and *strength* (that is, the body and its actions).

Some social psychologists tell us that not only do our attitudes
affect our actions, but our actions affect our attitudes. Sixteenth-
century Anabaptist leader Hans Denck had something of the same
thing in mind when he wrote that people cannot know Christ unless they follow him in life; nor can anyone follow him unless they
already know him. Mind and body, spirit and action, theology and
ethics are always connected. In the Gospel of John, Jesus says,
"They who have my commandments and keep them are those who
love me. . . . Those who love me will keep my word." (14:21-23).
What we do makes a difference spiritually.

Sometimes people involved in self-destructive behavior say, "If
it doesn't hurt anyone else, then it's okay for me to hurt myself."
Those who commit suicide also use this line of reasoning. What
they forget is that they are not their own; they belong to God, body
and soul.

Even as the church counsels against suicide as contrary to what
God wants, this needs to be done with God's love and compassion.
It is not helpful to be condemning at the funerals of suicide victims.
While we know that violence is wrong and suicide is wrong, we do
not know the mind of God, nor do we know the mind of the suicide victim at the time of death. Motives can be very complex, and
it is not for us to predict how God will treat anyone on the day of
judgment. We all stand in need of God's mercy.

Comment: Dealing with abuse

The Statement on Violence notes that "at the heart of nearly all violence in close relationships is the desire to control or use another
person." Violence often involves an imbalance of power in a relationship. In society as a whole, men have power over women (more
than 90 percent of spousal abuse is done by men against women).
Leaders have greater power than followers. Adults, especially parents and teachers, have power over children. Employers have
power. Pastors have power. When there is an imbalance of power, it
is easy for those with greater power to start thinking, "The rules
don't apply to me." Or, "I am special, so I should be able to get
around the rules." That is often when abuse of power occurs.

Healing from such abuse, especially when it involves physical or sexual abuse, does not begin with the simple message to the victim, "Go kiss and make up." Skilled intervenors in domestic violence invariably say that the first response must be to help the victim get to safety. Reconciliation cannot begin as long as perpetrators of violence are avoiding responsibility for their actions, or making excuses. Reconciliation, if it occurs, is usually a long, painful process. Forgiveness needs time to mature.

Plan possibilities

Break into small groups, each of which will discuss one of the following scenarios. The group will use its biblical reflection to come up with a response to the person in question.

1) A young woman who has come home from college and reported that she was raped by her date.
2) The father of a person who has committed suicide and now wonders about that person's salvation.
3) A 10-year-old boy in your congregation who has bruises and other signs of physical abuse.
4) An unmarried couple considering abortion.
5) A woman who says no to being on a church committee because her husband doesn't want her to be gone from home in the evenings, and who then confides to you that her husband has been beating her and slapping her around for "offenses" such as burning the dinner or coming home from work 20 minutes late.
6) A person abusing drugs who says, "If it doesn't hurt anyone else, it's okay."
7) A person who has difficulty controlling anger and once almost got into a fist fight at a congregational meeting.

The Statement on Violence has suggestions how the church might respond. Read the sections in bold italics, beginning with "*In response to violence against oneself, we call the church to . . .*" (page 6) and "*In response to violence in close relationships, we call the church to . . .*" (page 9) Which of these responses would be most helpful in the situations mentioned above? What other responses could you make?

Act on it

Option A

Before next session, think about a situation in which someone you know is having difficulty with self-inflicted violence, or with violence inflicted upon him or her by a spouse or other close relation. List practical ways in which your congregation or study group can be a safe place for such people. Will they know it's okay to get help with their problems, and that they will find forgiveness, healing, and a fresh start? What steps are needed for such a safe place to be created?

Option B

Find out what the church discipline procedures are in your congregation. What would happen with a person who confessed to the pastor, or deacons, or elders, or someone else that he or she was committing domestic violence?

For next time:
Read Sections III.C. and III.D. of the Statement on Violence.

Going deeper

Use one of the Mennonite Central Committee packets listed in the bibliography for further study. Packets are available on abortion, spousal abuse, child sexual abuse, and sexual abuse in professional relationships. Or watch the Mennonite Media Ministries video *Beyond the News: Sexual Abuse*.

Session 3
Violence in Leisure and Violence in Society

Reflect on your experience

Violence is not just an individual or personal problem. This session deals with violence in the media, in leisure, on the street, committed by individual strangers or in an institutionalized setting. Begin the session by reflecting on the four stories on pages 24-36: "Whose Responsibility?" "Threatened at Gunpoint," "Parents of Slain Prisoner Plead for Mercy for Their Son's Killer," and "Neighborhood Closes Second Crack House."

Assuming the group has read the stories ahead of time, reflect on all four stories as a group. What are the varieties of violence shown here? How did the persons in the stories respond to violence? If members have not read them, take time to read one or two, and reflect on the same questions.

Comment: "Redemptive" Violence in the Media

Most cartoon shows and many television shows and movies are based on the "myth of redemptive violence." This myth says that violence is bad when committed by the bad guys, but violence is okay if committed by good guys in response to the violence by the bad guys. (And we, of course, are always on the side of the good guys.) Confusing logic? Yes. But think about how many recent shows you have seen that operate on the principle that the only way to fight violence is with more violence.

Some moments in history when Mennonites as a group have been the victims of violence:

• The martyrdom of Anabaptists in Europe during the sixteenth century.
• The burning of churches and harassment during World War I, especially in Kansas and Oklahoma.
• Attacks against Mennonites during the Bolshevik Revolution and the Stalinist era. (Some congregations will have members who experienced this, or whose parents did.)
• Persecution of Ethiopian Mennonites in the 1980s.
• The burning of Indonesian Mennonite church buildings in the last few years.

Does watching all this make-believe violence make us behave more violently? Recent studies say yes. Dave Grossman, in his book *On Killing* (see bibliography), writes that research on wars historically has revealed that most soldiers did not shoot to kill. In some cases, dead soldiers were found with their rifles having never been shot. Or if forced to shoot, they shot to miss. In other words, the kill rates per shot fired were low, because there is a basic human desire not to kill other human beings.

When modern armies discovered this, they began using desensitization techniques in order to raise the kill rates. For example, they had soldiers practice shooting at targets that looked like people, rather than targets that were concentric circles. By the time of the Vietnam War, U.S. army kill rates were up. Grossman says that the increased amount of violence we see in movies and on television has the same desensitization effect on us. It makes us more likely to think of violence as business-as-usual, and it makes people more willing to commit violent acts themselves. Instead of violence-as-entertainment being cathartic (giving a safe outlet for violence), such violence in the media is rehearsal for doing violence.

Discuss: Where do we see an increase in violence in TV programs, movies, video games, and music lyrics? What is the effect on people? Does it make people more likely to want guns for personal protection?

What kinds of societal violence have we personally experienced? Hate crimes? Assaults by strangers?

Think biblically

Read and discuss Philippians 4:4-9. With what should we fill our minds? What does the passage say we should do in order for the God of peace to be with us? How does this relate to our entertainment choices? When should we not participate in violence as entertainment?

Read and discuss Acts 14. Here, the apostles Paul and Barnabas experience violence and threats of violence. How do they and the other disciples respond? Why? What effect does the violence have on the continuation of their missionary work?

Summarize: Go through the Scripture passages studied in this session and compile a list of helps for those who suffer violence for doing good.

Comment: Suffering for the right

In the New Testament, the violence against Christians is undeserved. Often violence against us, committed by strangers, is also undeserved. First Peter 4:1-2, 12-19 is explicit about the response Christians should have to violence against them: Believers should not be surprised at persecution. They should be willing to suffer as Christ did. If they are reviled for the name of Christ, they are blessed. "Therefore, let those suffering in accordance with God's will entrust themselves to a faithful Creator, while continuing to do good." In other words, it is better to suffer violence than to commit violence, even in self-defense or in retaliation against violence. This is what Paul did in Acts 14, after being nearly stoned to death. Rather than calling for vengeance on their enemies, Paul called the other disciples to continue in the faith because "It is through many persecutions that we must enter the kingdom of God" (Acts 14:22).

Plan possibilities

Many Christian peacemakers have chosen creative responses to violence or attempted violence instead of responding with violence in kind. One Mennonite woman working as a missionary in New York City's Bowery district early in this century had been passing out gospel tracts on the street. Shortly afterward she was confronted by a would-be robber. Refusing to be intimidated, she waved her briefcase (filled with tracts) at the robber and told him, "This case is filled with dynamite." The robber, not wanting to find out what kind of dynamite, spiritual or physical, left her alone.

The books *Safe Passage on City Streets* and *What Would You Do?* (see bibliography) give more recent examples of persons who turned away attackers nonviolently, often using an element of surprise to throw the attacker off guard. In one city, a group of churches, including Mennonite congregations, has sponsored prayer vigils at the sites of drive-by shootings.

Read and discuss: The bold italic sections of III.C. and III.D. in the statement (pages 11 and 12) offer some suggestions for application activities. Note that some of the activities are to be done in the home and in the church, while others activities involve public witness. Why is action in all three arenas important?

What witness against violence has your church made? Or how have individuals in the congregation witnessed against violence in society? From the list of responses in the Statement on Violence, which ones fit your congregation?

Act on it

Between now and the next session, make one response to violence in leisure and in public life. It may mean writing a letter to a public official, evaluating a TV show or computer game with your child, or some other activity inspired by today's section of the statement. Observe what difference this makes in you, or in someone else. Agree as a group that you will report on your responses at the next session.

Option

Before next session, read and consider the Disarmament Pledge described under Going Deeper (page 56). Be prepared to take some time next session to discuss whether your group or congregation could make this covenant together.

This activity will be more relevant to people in the United States, where owning handguns is legal, and using guns for personal protection is culturally approved. One approach for both Canadians and Americans would be to adapt the pledge to cover other kinds of violent self-defense.

For next time:
Read Section III.E. of the Statement on Violence.

To the session leader:
In preparation for the next session, contact organizations like Conscience Canada, the National Campaign for a Peace Tax Fund, Project Ploughshares, or Mennonite Central Committee peace offices. Find out how much your country is spending on the military (war and preparation for war), on interest on the national debt for past military expenditures, and military aid to other countries.

Going deeper

The Mennonite Central Committee U.S. office in Washington, D.C., has compiled a Gun Violence Study and Advocacy packet, a resource for individuals and groups.

This 40-page packet provides theological reflections on gun violence, information regarding gun violence and the gun control debate, stories from the Mennonite community of experiences with gun violence, and action suggestions for people wanting to reduce gun violence. One of the suggestions is the Disarmament Pledge (page 56). Signing the pledge can be the culmination of an educational event or Sunday school class using the packet to study this issue.

The Disarmament Pledge is one tool for people who want to affirm publicly that we put our faith not in guns but in the Lord. A copy of the pledge can be framed and displayed in a church's fellowship area, or even shared with the local newspaper or in another public forum. The community would take note that the congregation is applying the Bible's message of peace and nonviolence to our contemporary situation. It would be a way of publicly reaffirming our peace-church history and challenging the violent ways of the world.

It could also be a powerful advocacy tool. A copy of it can be sent to one's elected officials along with a letter urging support for gun control. A copy can also be sent to the MCC Washington Office. In turn, we will help keep people informed about public policies, initiatives and actions addressing gun violence.

MCC's perspective is that historic peace churches, such as the Mennonites, keep the peace witness alive through public actions that affirm and follow the nonviolent example of Jesus. Today when the viability of the church's peace witness is being questioned, we need to find new and effective ways to respond to the prevailing violence in our land. It is hoped the packet and pledge are two tools that help us do that.

Disarmament Pledge

The *Confession of Faith in a Mennonite Perspective* sets forth our belief that peace is the will of God. It further states that the same Spirit that empowered Jesus' ministry of peace and justice also empowers us to resist evil without violence and to witness against all forms of violence.

Of the many forms of violence in our country, gun violence is one of the most deadly. Ninety-nine Americans are killed with firearms every day; 14 of those are children. The epidemic of gun violence has fostered a culture of fear and death in our land.

In response I/we pledge to more fully utilize the power of nonviolence (through empathetic listening, gestures of love, truthtelling, prayer, etc.) and to seek to become more rooted in God's love, which has the power to transform persons and situations.

(For individuals and family) Additionally, as a disciple of Jesus Christ, who said, "Put away your sword," I pledge myself not to look to any lethal weapon for protection against attack. No gun for supposed protection will have a place in my home. I find my security in God who delivers.

Name _____
(can be signed by an individual, a married couple, or a family)

(For congregations or groups) Additionally, we pledge ourselves to live as disciples of Jesus Christ, having no weapons for protection but the weapons of the Spirit. We want our homes to be a zone of God's peace where physical weapons for supposed defense can have no place. God helping us, we would give our lives in protecting others, but from Jesus we know that we must never take the life of anyone.

Name_____
(pledge can be taken by congregation or group within congregation)

Date _____

(Please send a copy of this pledge, with your address, to the MCC Washington Office: 110 Maryland Ave. NE #502, Washington DC 20002. In turn, MCC will help keep you informed about public policies, initiatives, and actions addressing gun violence.)

Session 4
Global Violence

Reflect on your experience

Report on your responses to public violence and violence in entertainment since the last session. What did you do? What effect did it have on you? On others? What would you do differently next time? What follow-up is needed?

The next widening circle of violence is global violence, which we see most acutely in war. In contrast to much one-on-one violence or random violence, this violence between groups and nations is highly organized. Billions of dollars are spent training and preparing for war, or the threat of war. It is usually legal or unregulated by law. It is supported by a vast network of businesses that manufacture weapons and a vast bureaucracy of the armed forces that former U.S. President Dwight Eisenhower called the "military-industrial complex." War kills innocent civilians as well as soldiers; civilians are currently 90 percent of the total casualties of wars. The thousands of still-operable nuclear weapons threaten to destroy even larger numbers of people and the infrastructure of society. Land mines continue to kill civilians long after wars are officially over.

Discuss: What have been your experiences with war? With military service or conscientious objection to military service? What kinds of witness against war have you made?
How does society's approval of war and preparation for war contribute to a culture of violence?

After the arrest of Timothy McVeigh (a former U.S. soldier) for the bombing of the Oklahoma City federal building in 1995, some news commentators were asking, How could such a good soldier kill so many people? What is the connection between socially-approved military violence and socially-disapproved personal violence? What is the effect on poorer nations when U.S. and Canadian manufacturers export so many weapons of war, and scarce resources are spent on the military rather than on economic development or helping citizens of those nations meet basic human needs?

Think biblically

The Christian church of the early centuries did not approve of war or participation in war. They did not see how followers of Christ could take up the sword against enemies, even if ordered to do so by the government. Jews, and thereby Jewish Christians, were exempt from military service because the Roman army did not want soldiers who refused to work on the Sabbath. Slaves and women also were not eligible to serve as soldiers. Military service became an issue in the church as the church spread among freeborn Gentile men.

Read and discuss 1 Peter 2:9-25. In verse 11, what is the relationship of believers to the culture around them? How do they identify themselves (vv. 9-10)? How is one to treat the Roman emperor compared to how one treats "everyone" (v. 17), or compared to how one is to behave toward God? In what way is Jesus an example to those who suffer unjustly (vv. 18-25)? What does it mean concretely to "follow in his steps"?

The first-century church saw itself as a community of pilgrims and strangers (or aliens and exiles) within a hostile culture. How can we also be a community of peace in a culture of violence? How are we a community of pilgrims and exiles within the dominant culture in North America?

How should those of us who affirm our loyalty to the kingdom of God and to a God who loves enemies (see Romans 5:6-11) respond to military violence, especially when it is promoted by the government of the country in which we live?

Often during times of war, Mennonites and other peacemakers have been ridiculed, harassed, and persecuted because they refused to go to war or to buy bonds to pay for war. In Kansas and Oklahoma during World War I, persecution and criticism was especially severe. Barns and even a church building were burned. One Mennonite who refused to buy "liberty" bonds was almost lynched. Two Hutterite young men from South Dakota who refused to put on the military uniform were mistreated and died in military prison.

Plan possibilities

Read the story "Prayer on the Rooftop." How did Christian Peacemaker Teams in the West Bank work against violence?

Take a few minutes for each person to review the application ideas given in the statement, page 14, as well as the additional suggestions listed below. Make two lists on a sheet of paper: actions you have already taken, and actions that you could, practically, take right now. Of the second list, mark those that stretch your comfort level, and those that you may disagree with.

In the larger group, share one response activity that you have done, one that you would like to do, and one that stretches your comfort level. What are the barriers to implementing some of the new ones?

Additional actions against global violence

1. Some Christians historically have witnessed against global violence by:
   —refusing to join the military, even as a noncombatant.
   —refusing to pay taxes that are used for war and preparing for it.
   —avoiding work in military industries, making the weapons of war.
   —not investing in companies that make military hardware.
   —refusing to sing national anthems with military themes ("we stand on guard for thee" and "the rockets' red glare, the bombs bursting in air").
   —refusing to say the pledge of allegiance to the U.S. flag, just as early Christians refused to give the pinch of incense to Caesar. (This was the beginning of many Mennonite elementary schools in the eastern U.S., when public schools began requiring children to say the pledge of allegiance. Since that time, the U.S. Supreme Court has affirmed the right of any student to refuse to say the pledge of allegiance on religious grounds.)
   —refusing to sign loyalty oaths to governments.

2. Beyond the nonparticipation, Christians have also tried the following positive actions:
   —communicating with legislators and others in government.
   —working for passage of peace tax legislation through organizations such as Conscience Canada or the (U.S.) National Campaign for a Peace Tax Fund.
   —working to remove land mines, such as Mennonite Central Committee has done in Laos.
   —actively peacemaking in the midst of hostilities through organizations like Christian Peacemaker Teams.

Act on it

From Planning Possibilities, plan to do something before the next session as a witness against the violence of war. Write it on a piece of paper and share it with another person. Ask that person to ask you next week whether you have made the witness you said you would.

Session 5
Discipling toward nonviolence

Reflect on your experience

Tell some stories of your experiences with accountability in the church. How have others in the church discipled you or mentored you? What have you seen of church discipline in this congregation or in other congregations that you have been a part of? Was discipline practiced in a constructive way?

Organize yourselves into a line showing a continuum of the group's feelings on discipline in the church, based on your experiences. One end of the continuum would be "Church discipline is a good and necessary thing" and at the other, "Church discipline is always negative."

In this session we look at the issue of church discipline, since the topic often emerges as congregations attempt to deal lovingly with members whose behaviour may be violent, or who speak or act in support of various forms of violence.

Think biblically

Read and discuss Galatians 5:16–6:2. There are two lists here: the works of the flesh and the fruit of the Spirit. How do the works of the flesh (5:19-21) contrast with the fruit of the Spirit (5:22-23)? How would it be easy for those who are living by the Spirit to act with conceit toward those who aren't? How are they to act toward those who "are detected in a transgression" (6:1-2)?

Read and discuss Jude 17-23. Here again are descriptions, on the one hand, of "worldly people, devoid of the Spirit" and, on the other hand, the "beloved," to whom the author is writing. How are the "beloved" to treat those who are "devoid of the Spirit" (vv. 22-23)? Use this text to imagine different kinds of discipling responses to different kinds of sins in the community. What does it mean to exercise discipline with gentleness (Gal. 6:1) and mercy (Jude 22-23)?

Respond to the following comment:

In the context of the dominant culture's live-and-let-live attitude toward misconduct and the reluctance even to name sin "sin", why should the church discipline at all? Several reasons can be outlined:

1. We practice discipline because the church needs boundaries. Because we believe that knowing Jesus means following Jesus in life, behavior makes a difference. Part of the task of the church is to discern what kind of behavior is consistent with God's call, and what is not. Without boundaries, you don't know who you are, and new people looking at your congregation don't know who you are, either.

The problem with church discipline is that it can be used to regulate behavior that may not make much difference. A generation ago in some congregations, young rebels in the church wore neckties, whereas in most churches today young rebels would never be seen in a necktie. Skirt length and hair length, music styles and technology have all been the center of church discipline. In some intentional communities, leaders got caught up in supervising members' reading materials.

These examples show how easy it is to focus on the little things and miss the big picture. In church discipline, it is more important for the church to define the center than to define the boundaries. What is the direction toward which we all want to be moving? How can we encourage each other in obtaining that goal? Only in that context, realizing that none of us have reached the goal, should we then define the boundaries. The process of church discipline should, most of the time, be more like a magnet than a fence. A magnet defines the center and draws us toward it. A fence tells us whether we are in or out. Both are needed. But fence-oriented discipline without magnet-oriented discipline can yield harsh and arbitrary decisions.

2. We practice discipline because it continues the process of discipleship. Discipleship begins before baptism and continues throughout the Christian pilgrimage. Our whole life of faith is a process of becoming transformed into the image of Christ, and that process is communal, not just individual. Church discipline becomes part of the process after baptism, which marks a person's commitment to grow into greater faithfulness.

3. We practice church discipline because we love those who are caught in sin. In the case of those who have been committing violent acts, we want to help them get out of the mess they are in. We want them to stop hurting others. How is it possible to love someone and not try to keep them from committing violence against themselves or others? Friends don't let friends commit violence. Brothers and sisters in the church don't let brothers and sisters do harm.

4. *We practice church discipline because we need a clear witness in the world.* In the first century, people looked at Christians and said, "See how they love one another!" Can the same be said about the church today? It is difficult for a church to preach against violence in the world when the church appears to be unconcerned about violence among its members. We have to get our house in order.

Plan possibilities

Examine your church's way of helping people live nonviolently.

Either through a presentation by a congregational leader, or through a group study of your constitution or mission statement, explore the following:

- How central is peacemaking in your church's identity?
- In reaching out to newcomers, how quickly are they oriented to your position on peace and nonviolence?
- What is expected of members with regard to knowing about peace, and living out peace? How specific are these expectations?
- How does your church respond to soldiers or veterans wanting membership in the church? Are they expected to indicate willingness to be taught and nudged in new directions?
- Choose one or more of the violent acts mentioned in the statement. What would happen in your church if a member of your congregation committed this act or acts?
- How can we hold each other accountable in matters of peace and nonviolence, in a way that is full of grace and mercy?

Examine how you share your faith with others. Do you tell them not only that Jesus saves us from the sin we commit, but also from the sins that others commit against us, and from the need to retaliate against them? Do you tell people about the church's peace stance early on, or do you spring it on them later? Is it clear that peace is a main ingredient of the gospel, or does it seem like just the parsley on the casserole? What are some ways you can integrate a peace witness in your way of describing your faith?

When members take a different position ...

Some congregations have felt it helpful to ask, as a minimum commitment, that people agree to a statement something like this: I understand that this church sees peace and nonviolence as central to the gospel, and I agree to be open to moving in that direction in my Christian walk. I also agree not to publicly oppose this congregation's commitment to peace and nonviolence.

One congregation made it clear to its young people in the military that the congregation did not approve of military involvement. At the same time, however, members of the congregation sent cookies, care packages, cards and other indications of their love.

Act on it

Before your group moves to discernment on the next steps (Session 6), determine which of the following stages best describes your congregation. Once you have decided (you may need to vote), take note of the action plans for the next session. Note that Session 6 of this guide will be most useful for churches who are in stages 3 through 5.

Stage 1

We're in conflict over peace and violence issues. In the past, we never said much about peace before people joined the church, and now we have members who think peace is an optional part of the gospel or don't believe in peacemaking at all. How can we give a clear witness to the world, when we ourselves are in conflict over issues of violence and peacemaking?

Action: Plan further study and reflection on peace and conflict management. The 1995 statement "Agreeing and Disagreeing in Love" may be helpful. It is available from the offices of the General Boards in Newton, Kansas, and Elkhart, Indiana (see page 69). See bibliography, page 19.

Stage 2

We are for peace, but we are not sure whether church discipline or peace discipleship is a good idea. We just let members decide for themselves on issues of peace and violence, and we don't try to hold each other accountable.

Action: Do more Bible study on church discipline. Some good sources include: *Confession of Faith in a Mennonite Perspective*, Article 14, and Marlin Jeschke's book, *Disciplining in the Church*.

Stage 3

We only practice church discipline on the "big" issues. We need to learn loving ways to be accountable to each other that aren't prying, or punitive, or harsh.

Action: Practice loving accountability in small groups through spiritual pilgrimages and personal sharing as you begin discerning next steps in working against violence. It's okay not to have it all together as you decide on next steps in Session 6.

Stage 4

We are willing to be held accountable for our actions regarding peace and violence, but we need help training for peacemaking.

Action: You may want to work on the spiritual disciplines of peacemaking, using the Beatitudes (Matt. 5:1-12) as a beginning point. You'll find the next session helpful as part of the rhythm of reflection and action.

Stage 5

We have been united in working for peace, but we'd like to move farther along the path.

Action: You are ready for discerning further your peace witness in the world. See the next session.

For next session:

If you are going on to Session 6, please read the 42 action plans listed in the statement, pages 6-14. Note the ones to which you feel you and/or your church are being called.

Session 6
Next steps

Reflect on your experience

On newsprint or on the chalkboard, list answers to the following questions: What have you learned about violence and peacemaking? What do you still want to learn?

Think biblically

Read and discuss Matthew 5:1-16. Verses 2 through 11, known as the Beatitudes, contain several references to peace and nonviolence. In verse 5, the "meek" are really the "gentle," the "nonviolent." This Beatitude is a paraphrase from Psalm 37, which is about leaving vengeance toward the wicked in God's hands. In verse 6, the blessed are those who hunger and thirst for righteousness, which is also translated "justice." Verse 9 blesses peacemakers. Verses 10-12 suggests a response of rejoicing, not retaliation, in the face of persecution.

On a section of newsprint or the chalkboard, recall examples where peacemaking and nonviolence have been salt and light in the world.

Plan possibilities

Spend most of this session on the following process of prayerful discernment.

1. Survey possible directions. In the bold italic sections of the Statement on Violence are 42 "calls to the church" (pages 6-14). Obviously not every group or even every congregation can do all of these things. God does not call us to do everything at once. But we can listen to God's call to *us now*. These "calls" fall into five broad categories (listed in the conclusion of the statement, page 15):

1. Commit ourselves to be communities of nonviolence, church communities that demonstrate a peaceful alternative to violence.

2. Teach nonviolence and peacemaking, both within the church and beyond it.

3. Confront, in the Spirit of Jesus Christ, the powers, structures, institutions, and spirits violence that tend to shape human behavior.

4. Love both victims of violence and perpetrators of violence.

5. Renounce the use of violence and urge others to pledge to do the same.

Read through the list of suggested actions, noting the ones you feel especially called to pray about. What others might you want to add to the list? On the chalkboard or sheet of newsprint, list all the possible actions the group wants to consider. Group them, if appropriate. Give ample time to clarify what each means.

Option: If the group is large, you may want to break into groups for this activity. The groups might be divided along the lines of the five categories listed above (1-5), with persons joining the group whose category of action they feel drawn to.

2. Prepare your heart. Before working further on action plans, take a few minutes of silence to receive God's call. If you learn mainly by hearing, God's call may come through words—in a phrase, a quotation, or a line from a song. If you learn mainly by seeing, God may speak through a visual image. Such pictures are sometimes symbolic, and need interpretation. Sometimes they are are literal; you may see yourself acting against violence in a particular way. If you learn by feeling, touching, or moving your muscles, you may want to pray with your hands, palms up, to receive what God wants to give you.

During these quiet moments, clear your mind of preoccupations you may have brought to the session: the roast in the oven, the activity to which you need to take a child tomorrow, the meeting at work, the worries about your extended family, etc. Think of your mind as a stage. Do not try to push these other things off the stage, just watch them walk across the stage and then off. When all these things and people have walked off the stage, then begin listening and watching for what God wants to tell you or show you.

3. Pray. Spend 15 minutes together in silence, praying through listening, watching, and feeling. Pray, asking God to help you discover God's call to you now, regarding violence and peacemaking.

4. Share what you have received. In the group, talk about what you heard, saw, or felt during your prayer time. Share the intensity of the image, the word, the feeling. Was it a small nudge, or was it a strong call? Listen for common themes in the group. How does God seem to be leading you? Are there one or two actions that this group seems to be called to take?

5. Test your call. Is it in sync with the message of the Bible, especially as we know it through Jesus Christ? Does it make sense? Does it address the context in which you are living? Talk to others in the group; can they affirm this call? What risks are required of you? Are you willing to take these risks, and how can others help you take the risks? What kind of encouragement and help do you need in order to act on this call?

If you have more than one or two action calls that you feel called to, this is also a time to prioritize. Which ones are most important right now? Which ones can be worked on later?

Act on it

By now, you should have one or two action ideas in mind. (If you have more, you may want to prioritize them.) Decide on next steps. Who will do what? how? when? where? Take another session, if necessary, to work on implementing your action plans.

Close the session and the series with a time of worship and commissioning.

Option

Send the conclusions of your discernment process or comments about what you learned during the process to:

Mennonite Church General Board *or* **General Board**
Suite 600   **General Conference**
421 South 2nd Street   **Mennonite Church**
Elkhart, IN 46514   **P.O. Box 347**
E-mail: mcgb@juno.com   **Newton, KS 67114**
                                              E-mail: shelleyb@gcmc.org